D1551939

WILMA MANKILLER

Native American Leader

Emily Rose Kucharczyk

BLACKBIRCH PRESS

Detroit • New York • San Diego • San Francisco
Boston • New Haven, Conn. • Waterville, Maine
London • Munich

Published by Blackbirch Press
10911 Technology Place
San Diego, CA 92127
e-mail: customerservice@galegroup.com
Web site: http://www.galegroup.com/blackbirch

© 2002 Blackbirch Press
an imprint of the Gale Group

Printed in China

10 9 8 7 6 5 4 3 2 1

Photo credits:
Cover inset, page 22 © Tom Gilbert; pages 3, 16, 20, 24-25, 27 © Property of Blackbirch Press; page 4 © Storer's Cards, Inc.; page 6 © Museum of the American Indian; page 7, 15 © North Wind Picture Archives; page 6, 7, 17, 28, 30 © CORBIS; page 12, 13 © United States Department of Labor; page 10 © University of Arkansas; page 18, 47 © Dan Agent/Cherokee Nation; page 19 © courtesy of Cherokee Nation; page 29 © The White House

Library of Congress Cataloging-in-Publication Data
Kucharczyk, Emily Rose.
Wilma Mankiller / Emily Rose Kucharczyk.
      p. cm. — (Famous women juniors)
Includes index.
Summary: Describes the life of the Cherokee woman who overcame many hardships to become an activist and leader of her people, even serving as the first woman Principal Chief of the Cherokee Nation.
     ISBN 1-56711-593-4 (alk. paper)
1. Mankiller, Wilma Pearl, 1945 — Juvenile literature. 2. Cherokee women—Biography—Juvenile literature. 3. Cherokee Indians—Politics and government—Juvenile literature. [l. Mankiller, Wilma Pearl, 1945- 2. Cherokee Indians—Biography. 3. Indians of North America—Biography. 4. Women—Biography.]
I. Title. II. Series.
E99.C5 M3344 2002
973'.049755—dc21
                                                    2001005125

Wilma Mankiller was the first woman to become chief of the Cherokees. She has spent her life teaching others about Native Americans and helping Native Americans.

Wilma was born in Tahlequah, Oklahoma, in 1945. At that time, Tahlequah was a meeting place for Cherokees. People spoke the Cherokee language. Many street signs were in Cherokee. The only transportation was a train that stopped in town. Few people owned cars.

The Cherokee Alphabet

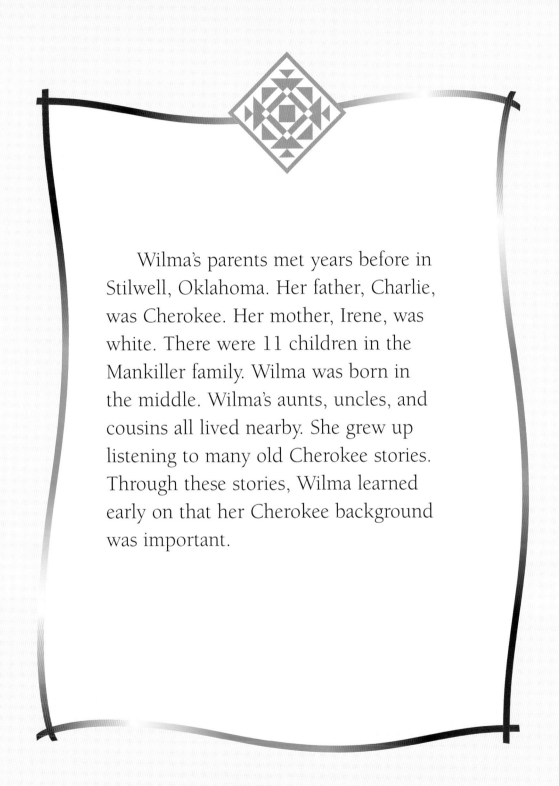

Wilma's parents met years before in Stilwell, Oklahoma. Her father, Charlie, was Cherokee. Her mother, Irene, was white. There were 11 children in the Mankiller family. Wilma was born in the middle. Wilma's aunts, uncles, and cousins all lived nearby. She grew up listening to many old Cherokee stories. Through these stories, Wilma learned early on that her Cherokee background was important.

The Cherokee in America

Life for the Cherokee in the 1940s was not easy. In fact, Native Americans had been mistreated for hundreds of years. When white settlers first arrived in America, the Cherokee were one of the most powerful tribes. Most Cherokee lived in what are now the states of Virginia, North Carolina, South Carolina, Georgia, Tennessee, and Alabama. The tribe had its own traditions. In 1821, a Cherokee named Sequoya had even created a Cherokee alphabet to write their language.

Sequoya created the Cherokee alphabet.

Right: The U.S. government forced many native peoples off their traditional lands.

Below: The Treaty of New Echota gave Cherokee lands to white settlers.

CONSTITUTION

OF THE

CHEROKEE NATION,

MADE AND ESTABLISHED

AT A

GENERAL CONVENTION OF DELEGATES,

DULY AUTHORISED FOR THAT PURPOSE.

AT

NEW ECHOTA,

JULY 26, 1827.

As more white people moved to the continent, the Cherokee formed a tribal state for protection. But when gold was found on Cherokee land in 1828, whites moved in. Soon the U.S. government forced the Cherokees to move to Oklahoma. Many died on the way to Oklahoma. Life in the new land was hard for the tribe. By the time Wilma was born, the Cherokee had lived in Oklahoma for 100 years.

Wilma moved to San Francisco with her family when she was 11 years old.

A New Life

Wilma grew up learning about the mistreatment of her people. Then, when she was 11, a new U.S. government program was started to improve life for Native Americans. The Bureau of Indian Affairs controlled the program. It moved Native American families into cities where they could find work. So, in 1957, the Mankiller family left Stilwell and moved to San Francisco, California.

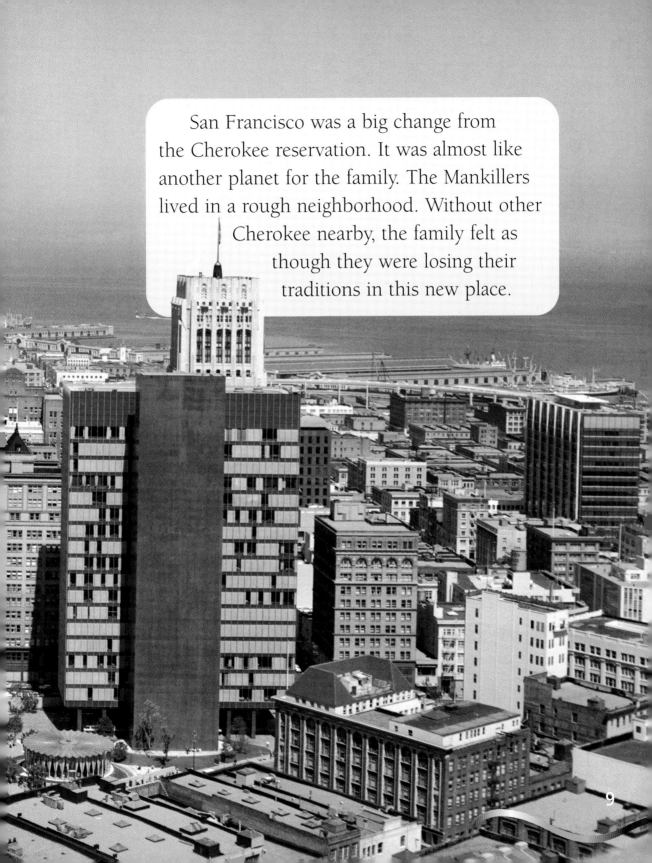

San Francisco was a big change from the Cherokee reservation. It was almost like another planet for the family. The Mankillers lived in a rough neighborhood. Without other Cherokee nearby, the family felt as though they were losing their traditions in this new place.

Wilma also began to lose hope of a better life. She spent many years in San Francisco. She went to high school there. Soon after graduating, she married Hector Olaya. In 1964, their first daughter was born. They named her Felicia. In 1966, Wilma's second daughter, Gina, was born. Then, in 1971, Wilma's father died from kidney disease.

In 1972, Wilma went to San Francisco State University to learn about social welfare programs. Social welfare programs help communities improve by showing people there how to help themselves.

Wilma attended San Francisco State University to learn about social welfare programs.

Wilma found it difficult to care for her children while going to school. Being a mother and student hurt her relationship with Hector, too. In 1974, Wilma and Hector were divorced. Through all her troubles, Wilma continued to work hard at school. She hoped to learn how to help other Native Americans.

Back in Oklahoma

In 1976, Wilma returned to Oklahoma. But she had not finished her college courses yet, so she could not find a job. After six months she went back to California. In 1977, she returned to Oklahoma again and began working for the Cherokee Nation.

Wilma's first job was getting young Native American students to enroll in a national environmental studies program. The U.S. Department of Labor ran the program. Its goal was to train Native Americans to solve environmental problems on their reservations.

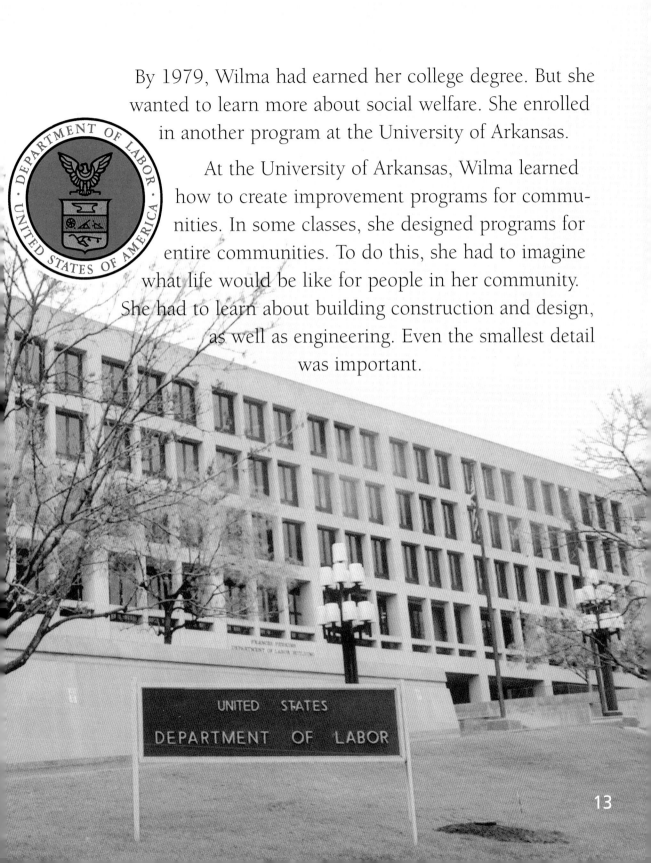

By 1979, Wilma had earned her college degree. But she wanted to learn more about social welfare. She enrolled in another program at the University of Arkansas.

At the University of Arkansas, Wilma learned how to create improvement programs for communities. In some classes, she designed programs for entire communities. To do this, she had to imagine what life would be like for people in her community. She had to learn about building construction and design, as well as engineering. Even the smallest detail was important.

UNITED STATES
DEPARTMENT OF LABOR

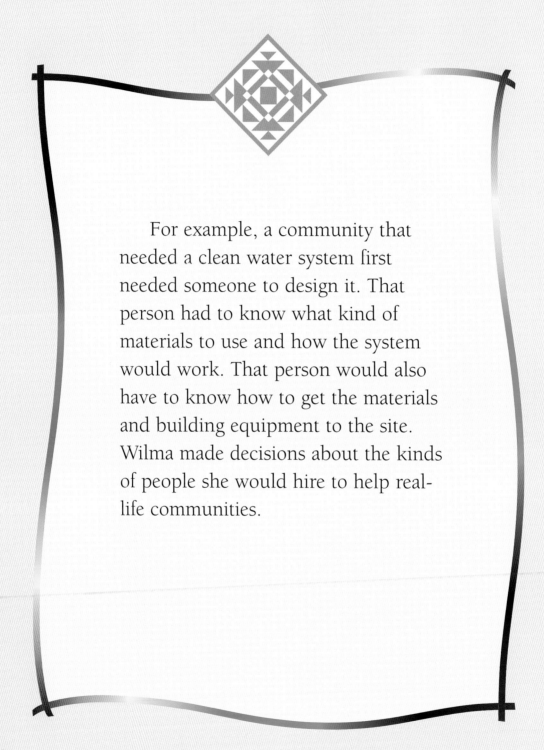

For example, a community that needed a clean water system first needed someone to design it. That person had to know what kind of materials to use and how the system would work. That person would also have to know how to get the materials and building equipment to the site. Wilma made decisions about the kinds of people she would hire to help real-life communities.

Soon after starting at the University of Arkansas, she was in a car accident. Driving home from classes one day, she crashed into another car. Wilma was almost killed and had to have many operations. The accident changed how she felt about life. Given another chance at life, she became even more involved with helping other people.

Wilma attended the University of Arkansas.

Building a Community

Before Wilma started any projects, she had to make people in the community believe that they could help themselves. "The single most important part of my work was trying to get people to maintain a sense of hope . . . and to see that they could come together and actually, physically change their community," she said.

Wilma decided to use her knowledge to help the Cherokee Nation.

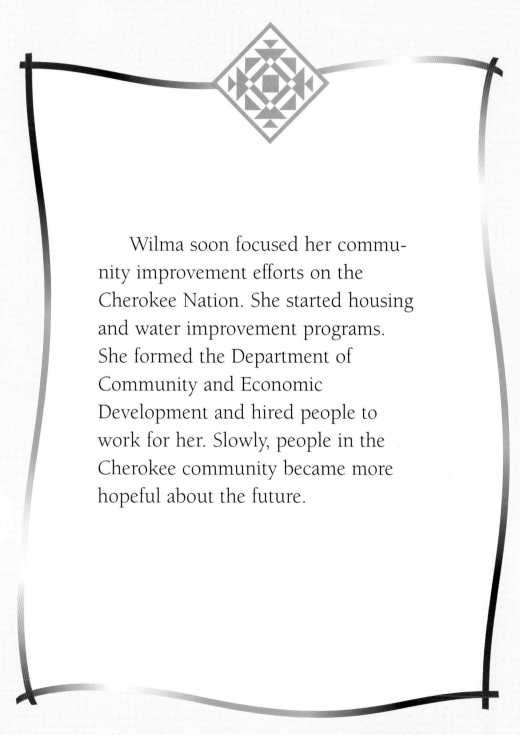

Wilma soon focused her community improvement efforts on the Cherokee Nation. She started housing and water improvement programs. She formed the Department of Community and Economic Development and hired people to work for her. Slowly, people in the Cherokee community became more hopeful about the future.

At the same time, Wilma had some problems of her own. In 1980, she found out that she had myasthenia gravis, which is a disorder of the nervous system. Wilma had a positive attitude about her health, however. And after years of medical treatment, the disorder went away. She said fighting the disease made her even more focused on life.

In the early 1980s, Wilma had a new mission—to help the community of Bell, Oklahoma. About 110 Cherokee families lived in the small town and most were poor. Many did not have indoor plumbing. Some people hunted for food to eat. Many of the town's problems were settled with violence.

Wilma had hope for the town. She noticed that Bell's people liked to share and help each other out. She believed an improvement project would be a success.

Wilma and her friend Charlie Soap took charge of the project. Wilma formed a group to help build a 16-mile water pipeline. Soon the townspeople had water to use in their homes and for farming. The people in the community learned that they could work together to make things better. They had a sense of pride in their community.

Wilma and her friend Charlie Soap worked together on the Bell improvement project.

The Next Step

After helping in Bell, Wilma was well known and popular. Many people thought she should run for political office. At first, Wilma wasn't sure she wanted to run for office. She did not feel comfortable asking people to vote for her. She did not like the idea of making speeches that explained her programs. On the other hand, she thought, getting elected would give her more power to make decisions for her people.

Wilma had to campaign for her position in the Cherokee Nation government.

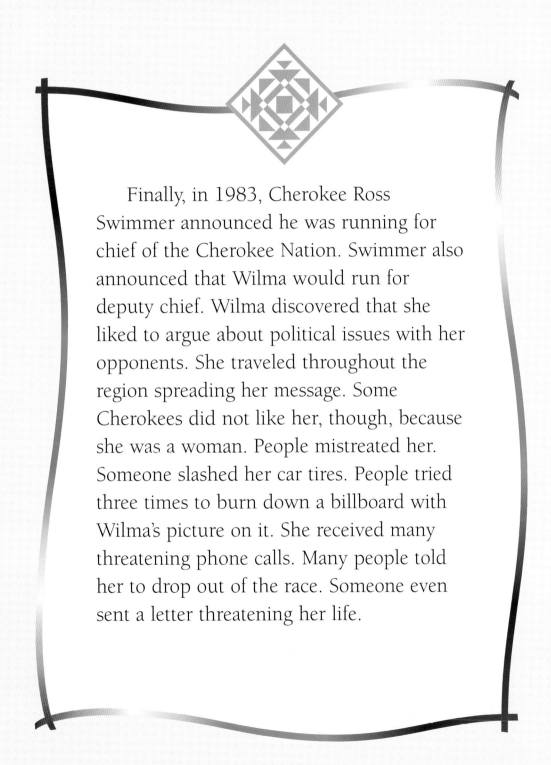

Finally, in 1983, Cherokee Ross Swimmer announced he was running for chief of the Cherokee Nation. Swimmer also announced that Wilma would run for deputy chief. Wilma discovered that she liked to argue about political issues with her opponents. She traveled throughout the region spreading her message. Some Cherokees did not like her, though, because she was a woman. People mistreated her. Someone slashed her car tires. People tried three times to burn down a billboard with Wilma's picture on it. She received many threatening phone calls. Many people told her to drop out of the race. Someone even sent a letter threatening her life.

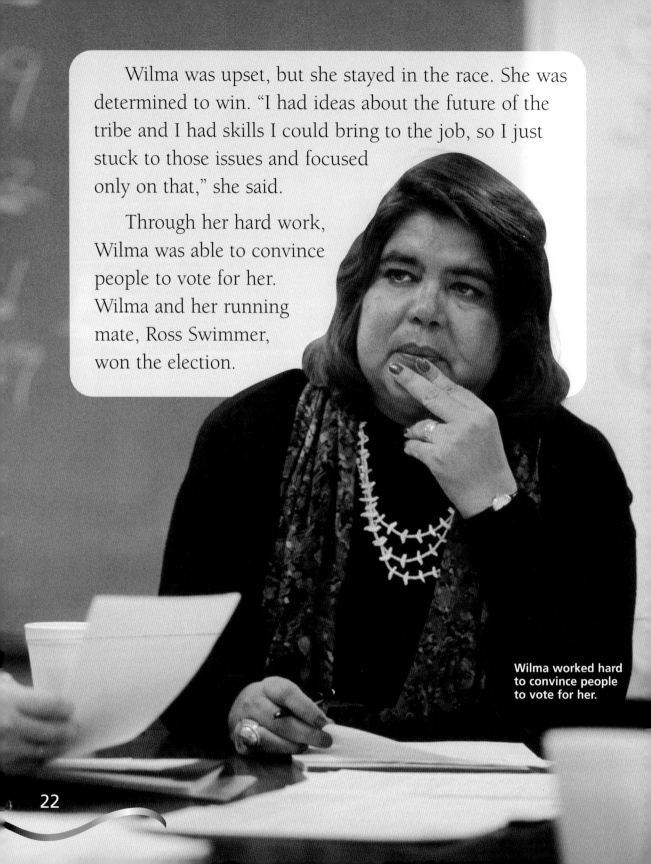

Wilma was upset, but she stayed in the race. She was determined to win. "I had ideas about the future of the tribe and I had skills I could bring to the job, so I just stuck to those issues and focused only on that," she said.

Through her hard work, Wilma was able to convince people to vote for her. Wilma and her running mate, Ross Swimmer, won the election.

Wilma worked hard to convince people to vote for her.

As deputy chief, Wilma was a high-ranking official in the Cherokee Nation. Many people, however, still focused on the fact that she was a woman. In her position, Wilma learned about politics, power, and how to get things done. In 1984, after Wilma's first year as deputy chief, her daughter Felicia gave birth to a baby boy. His name was Aaron Swake. Wilma was now a deputy chief—and a grandmother.

Wilma faced another change in 1985. Ross Swimmer was offered a job with the Bureau of Indian Affairs in Washington, D.C. When he took the job, Wilma became the principal chief of the Cherokee Nation. She became the group's top leader.

Many reporters wrote stories about Wilma because she was the first woman Cherokee chief. Soon people all over the United States learned about her and the Cherokee people. Many non-Indians thought that Native Americans hated America. By reading about Wilma, they learned that they were wrong to feel that way. White Americans also learned that Indians were good at working together and that they respected the environment.

The next year, 1986, Wilma married Charlie Soap. Also that year, Wilma received many awards and was elected to the Oklahoma Women's Hall of Fame. She was voted American Woman of the Year as well.

In 1987, Wilma's term as chief was up. She ran for the office again. There were still some people who were against Wilma because she was a woman. But during her first term she had run several programs that helped many Cherokees. People liked her work. Many voted for her, and she won.

Wilma worked at the Cherokee Nation headquarters in Talequah, Oklahoma.

One important goal Wilma had as chief was to get people to believe in themselves. She said many Native Americans felt helpless. For many years, the U.S. government had taken away the Indians' government, land, and culture. Many Native Americans lost confidence in their abilities and their beliefs. With Wilma's help, they learned that they can solve their own problems and better their lives.

Wilma has worked to improve the lives of poor Native Americans.

Wilma has a modern lifestyle, just like most Americans.

Wilma also spread her message in other countries. She believes that many people do not understand Native American culture and have false ideas about how Indians act and live. Some people in other countries thought that, because Wilma is a Cherokee, she rode to work on a horse. She actually drives a car. Others think she lives in a tepee, but she really lives in a house.

Wilma has worked hard to teach people what Native Americans are really like. Everywhere she goes she gives the same message: Native Americans are not poor and helpless. They have a beautiful and special culture. They work hard. And if people give them a chance, Native Americans can improve their lives. Wilma hopes that through her message, people will understand Native Americans and want to help them.

Wilma attended a meeting with Indian leaders and President Ronald Reagan in 1988.

Wilma's Work Today

Wilma is very proud of her work. She has helped several communities and brought many people together. Nothing has stopped her determination.

In 1990, she had a kidney transplant. Only a few weeks after the surgery, she was back at her desk ready to work. She has worked on setting up a Cherokee court system to settle arguments over land. She has also helped form a tax commission to look into ways for the tribe to make money.

In 1991, Wilma was elected to her second full term as chief. She got 83 percent of the vote. Wilma was very popular in Oklahoma and the Midwest. Many politicians in Washington, D.C. knew who she was. In January 1993, she participated in U.S. President Bill Clinton's inauguration. Later that year, she published a book about herself.

Wilma visits with U.S. Senator Daniel Inouye.

Wilma participated in the inauguration of President Bill Clinton.

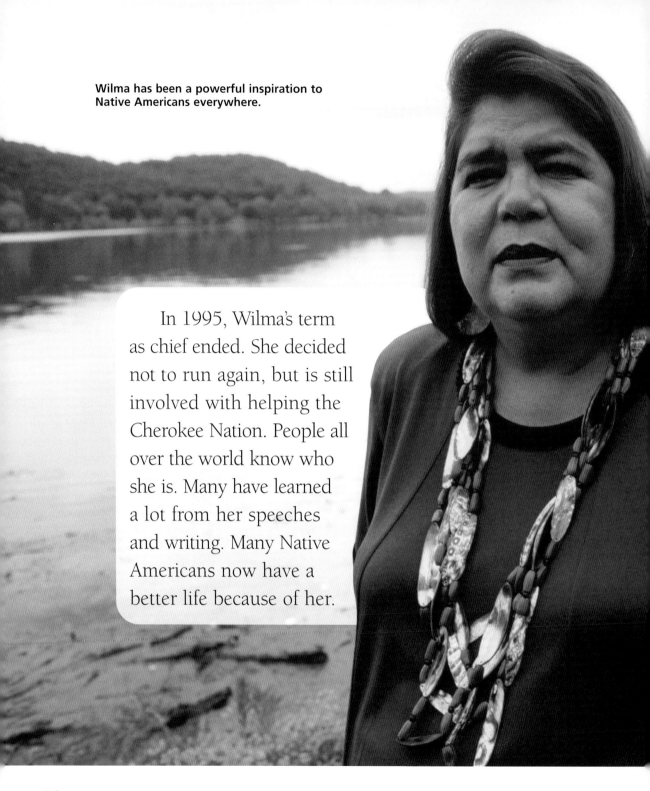

Wilma has been a powerful inspiration to Native Americans everywhere.

In 1995, Wilma's term as chief ended. She decided not to run again, but is still involved with helping the Cherokee Nation. People all over the world know who she is. Many have learned a lot from her speeches and writing. Many Native Americans now have a better life because of her.

Glossary

Community A group of people with shared interests and concerns.

Reservation A piece of land set aside by the government exclusively for Native Americans.

Settlers People who set up a community in a region before anyone else.

Tradition An inherited or repeated system of beliefs, actions, and behaviors.

Tribe A group of people who have common character, occupation, or interest: a political division.

For More Information

Websites

Wilma Mankiller: Powersource Gallery
www.powersource.com/gallery/people/wilma.html

This website offers a photo of Mankiller and biographical information.

The Cherokee Nation: Official Website
www.cherokee.org

Official site of the Cherokee Nation: includes extensive information on Cherokee news and customs, as well as speeches made by former Cherokee Chief Wilma Mankiller.

Books

Holland, Gini. *Wilma Mankiller (First Biographies)*. Austin, TX: Raintree/Steck-Vaughn, 1997.

Lowery, Linda. *Wilma Mankiller (Carolrhoda on My Own Book)*. Minneapolis: Carolrhoda, 1996.

Schwartz, Melissa. *Wilma Mankiller: Principal Chief of the Cherokees*. Broomall, PA: Chelsea House, 1995.

Index